THE SHORT LIFE OF
THE FIVE MINUTE
DANCER

THE SHORT LIFE OF

THE FIVE MINUTE

DANCER

by

Barry Wallenstein

7/20/93

for Jim + Sarah —

friedship —

love
Bay

Ridgeway Press
Detroit, Michigan

POETRY BY BARRY WALLENSTEIN

Beast Is A Wolf With Brown Fire

Roller Coaster Kid

Love and Crush

ISBN 1-56439-028-4

Published by The Ridgeway Press
P.O. Box 120
Roseville, MI 48066

Publisher: M.L. Liebler

In memory of my mother, Pearl Squires Wallenstein

CONTENTS

I. DARK SPECK DRIFTING

A Wonderful Change

Earlier I was a tree.
In fretful old age
troublesome insects worried my branches.
My roots were deep,
but the leaves were drying.

When I was a tree I said
here comes trouble to my boughs.
Now I'm a wood worm; my mind is a pin —
and though my life be brief,
I'm ageless and gay in the woods.

The Short Life of the Five Minute Dancer

I'm six hours absent all day long
like a weasel in winter in a tree,
deaf to the world:
I drift in the haze, latent, secretive,
absently waiting to dance and do
for five minutes at a time.
You, my doctor,
watch me last
for five minutes at a time.

Then watch me fade into
the six hour haze.
Sniff the way I breathe.
Deep in the haze I'm fine,
so fine in fact I'm fed through veins.

Now watch again closely:
I'm the dark speck drifting in the luminous sky,
the sudden recognition that all is not well,
the restive hour that spends the day,
the thing that will not scare
until —
I burst out to dance
for five minutes.
I last the while in the grandest style,
you — you watch me do
for five minutes at a time.

The Dream; The Flight

What is this dream
he's so tied into
that he can't see the rip in the sky,
can't feel its upward pull?

Asleep, he sails high
above the electric city
towards the black velvet flaps
and the darker inside.
He's not dressed for the flight
away from his usual punctualities.

The dream sticks,
but beneath its hidden drama
he feels that wherever he's drawn to,
whether it be a chamber of new delight
or a cracked egg with sulphurous walls,
he'll be set down gently,
awakened surely,
and he'll remember the coat and hat
he'd planned to wear
before the strange wind drilled him skyward.

Some Darkness

I want some darkness but
I'm not sure how much.

None, I'm sure
under the eyelids,
very little,
I'd like to believe,
shading the food I still need.

At night
and many times during the day
I like to crumple
into a pocket
of liquid darkness
and push my fingers
deep under my arms.

The darkness I dream of
is total and temporal
like a wash
or a spray of ink.

duck

You run around the corner
in new york city,
and in front of our eyes
there is the improbable pond.

My eyes blaze,
I've been told, in liquid,

and you, fearless and depressed
step into the pond
as a changeling duck,
darting your yellow bill
like a bobbin
as if looking for something you lost.
You give it up,
smile your duck smile, and
slowly quack out this story:

>"There was a swan one day went walking—
>came upon a frog;
>together they glided,
>and hoped to find
>a comfortable spot near the edge
>of the perfect pond.
>And they did.
>Both were happy but impossible;
>they couldn't make love
>so they talked about the outside world—
>and oceans:
>
>'Imagine' said the swan, 'we are a body of water,
>and as large objects fall on us
>we don't, of course, break, but
>undulate, rise and fall
>in a gentle flood.' "

Then you, the talker, the proverbial duck,
change into dry clothes
and both ponds vanish,
and, quick, before the night falls,
I stop seeing the same things you do.

Like Fools

You build the house so solid,
then, like fools, you ram it hard,
or burn it down.

See in the mirror,
shadows of flames—
black and white
wriggling against the fence;
your faces
backing away from all you've made,
drifting past what was a house,
a fence.

Like two arrows made of water,
you target two separate pools.

Apples

Susan and Mike enfold
after a long and tedious rift;
the water returns,
restructuring the sea.

At the mill
there is a fragrance of motion.
Mike working with the boys
turning the wheel,
the apples tumbling into pulp,
the pulp pressed into cider.

Every day now,
Susan forgets she is an American
Susan forgets she is Susan
and reddens others' faces
like apples, before being bitten
and left in the sun.

Mike remembers duller days,
days without sweaty Susan.

Rest now
wake up!

Like a Flea

One time I landed on the back
of one kind hand shaking another.
Maybe I was noticed, maybe not;
anyway, a friendship developed
and I was joined
throughout the season.

I never saw their eyes,
and that placed me
in a world of error.
Missing the glint
of certain entitlement,
I was let drop
in a new way.

The Old Man

From his watery eyes
to his pudding knees,
the Old Man
is not — has long been not —
a rubber ball in the hands of
that boy or that girl.

He is not a grave
nor, at this time of evening,
is he a wedding —
the guests cavorting,
forgetting everything, where
soldiers, in the distance, stand watch
as the village sleeps;
the young men snoozing in their lovers' arms.

He is not yet debris, piling
miles from the playground.

His brain is healthy grey.
It flashes, travels faster
than the boy's pitch
or the girl's laughter.
Listen: the mind twangs like an arrow,
it sounds like an ocean.

There is salt in the air
and he moves towards it.

In Case You Missed It

here it comes again:

The man walked across the bridge
very slowly
—like a star moving
against a ribbon
in the sky—
very long, the bridge, it was
very high
and the wind rolling along his back,
flapping at his coattails,
snapping against his trousers.

The iron railings are cold
and he avoids holding on
lest his hands freeze and stick.
He leans over the rail
he leans and stares
at the black invitation
flowing and churning—as if
there were a motor beneath
and an army of operators
all with families
working under the water
for pleasure;
he hears a promise

before—in the air

in case you missed it.

Kafka Blah Blah

He was pushed to the wall
for no wrong done
and the wall pressed hard,
scarred his palms
and burned apart his will.
Nothing: no voice, gruff or heard,
said a word
and there he was
as if invented for the day,
isolated, without effect, from
the riflemen he wouldn't count.

He knew his mouth was free,
and knowing these men knew death
as a habit
he bellowed
STABLEHANDS
and the great range of rifles
deep in harmony, laughed,
liking the knowledge,
changing the knowledge around.
But not the captain,
Mr. Chief of Occasions,
he barked, frothed and finally
whispered
"Keep him alive awhile
fire at the edges"
and with these words he disappeared
and the man's life against the wall took heat:
drifting in and out
he found himself seriously down.
From the bird's eye view
he looked fetal,
as he dreamed backwards
into his first and early hours

and upwards through his ages
and closer than ever came
every face, every delectable.

Grim Presence

My one grim friend
with the grudge of a nation
12 times defeated,
how did I earn your attention?
Somehow, sadly,
I got caught in your eye.

Here I am
helpless on your pupil,
and I don't like it!
If I could also be
the cotton swab to gently remove
the agonizing speck I've become,
how glorious and delivering
that would be.

Snowfire

Evening again!

> In mid-January
> somewhere
> by the side of a country road
> a small fire smolders in the snow
> left now by the men
> who had come to cut branches
> the small fire burns
> abandoned, pictorial and useless.

While I huddle to the wall for warmth
and curse my luck
miserable the cold
couldn't get worse.

> Somewhere
> a bluejay is barely seen against the snow
> meadows without footprints
> somewhere a fire in the hearth
> warm and easy conversation.

But what do they know of beauty
what do they know of the
twist on the tooth
that makes the pain
that blinds the eyes
that need to see
what to take
to ease the pain?

> Somewhere
> I can make it out
> a cow is grazing
> many cows are grazing
> there's a separate field up the road
> where 17 Black Angus cattle make a picture.

But what do they know of beauty
they turn away from the fire
they talk about how severe the weather is
damn skull tooth and white stone
I'll make better sense in my corner
than all the sunsets seen by clibber clabber
    by all those damn clibber clabbers
    who hang out   out
    out there.

Tears
   (for David Rosenthal)

There are tears in the water
the water can't fathom;
the fish, the reptiles,
the larger clans, are all disturbed;
distanced from themselves,
they fall dumb.

Off to the side
I build a casket.
Others of my kind wait, tensing,
and when the wind strikes the vane
they weep in profusion.

What melts in the sea
and settles so deeply?

What soft cloth,
wrapped round the head of the boy,
will cushion his gentle recline?

The Life of a Mole

There are moles burrowing,
making their way,
silently riding, scurrying, gliding
on glistening claws.
Faced by a box, they hesitate.
But soon, the texture is familiar,
with an odd taste fleeting, after.
And then there are the brass handles.

Apart from yet near to
these craven, careless, chewing creatures
and their startled eyes,
there are other eyes, quiet,
staring through, canceling out
the channeling moles.

The Missing Person

Every time there's a photo of 3 people
some invisible presence, fleet & vague,
not quite God, but of his ilk,
knows which one of the 3 will drop out first.
He knows the date of departure,
the name and gesture prior to leaving.

But there's a check on what he knows,
such as the whereabouts of the other 2
or their dates or even if they knew—
know to grieve or miss or wonder about
their old friend who stood with them
and looked at the camera as they did
that time.

Folks posing for pictures—he smiles
on his way out of town.

The waves of the dead
that sometimes gather in storms
and whip about on the high seas
and onto the shores
grinding stones into stones. . .

STOP!

The missing person from the photo
reappears as a surfer
cresting a giant foamy wave,
gliding safely to the shore;
the sun poised for one of those everlasting afternoons

in a box
which is a theater
with a silver screen.

Echoes

Every something is the echo of
nothing. — John Cage

A new idea: the edge of a ripple
belongs to the splash on the lake
the tossed stone made.
And the idea too is that stone.

There is a new smile
seen down the hallway.
The camera zooms the distance
and all along the way
faces are smiling on the walls
teaching smiles
of a copy of a copy of

who said what/when
up to this moment
who bent over this way
after saying hello to someone
before falling in love
and having an argument
or after some battle
(echoes of the cave age)
or making up
(echoes of Hollywood)
as in EMBRACE.

The ebullient heart
feels more than just the smacking kiss.
It wants to stick and quiver.
It needs to be caused
from afar.

NOTHING again—
so famous and sure of itself
is echoing upward—

Mother

1.

the morning after mother died
my mouth tasted metal
my breath turned foul
a week later I blew a kiss
at her grave and the grave-flowers died
the moon browned above me
and I felt her fall more deeply downwards

2.

before this happened mother was first
in one place and then in another
always limited however concentrated
now she's everywhere a film of power
father's abandoned
while she spills her favors like stardust
equally on all of us who think

3.

my children just wandered out of sight
far down the park's lane
mother watch them for me
grandmother you are don't doze
don't be too still
I trust them to come back
slightly more than I don't trust
the park
to let them return

II. WITH OUR LANGUAGE AND POWER

Dialectic

There's a knowing greater than telling.
I've seen it.
It wiggles not at all.
That is, it seems of a straight line.

Telling won't help
Worship straight lines
and you'll surely botch your circles.

Us

What can we do on this planet?
Strike a match, for example.
We shake it out, without thinking.
We can keep the fire from posing a danger.
We can toss a stick
seven times the length of our bodies
and still feel small,
let's say, or creative.
We can consider how deep or high the fire can go.
There are holes in the ground.

And we swat flies
in offices high up in cities
or in squat huts—
military or civilian.
The buzzing creatures flatten to stains
and we, with our language and power,
go down like flies
every time the rules of the righteous are broken.

In Air

The tire is flat—again,
the third time this week
and the carburetor's clogged
with gum, and
a cousin I've loved for 100 years
has just died   alone
no one knew.

My breath still fogs a winter window
this winter so far.
I motivate in the air
I love, down to the motes.

On an Alpine hill
another streaks down the course,
a red blur against the pines,
a healthy swish.

If I could, I'd ask her
what she knows about Calcutta,
Rangoon, old toothless men
who fought in the Great War
and slipped into the '60's
for a minute,
before her glad time
skiing downhill.

She is panting,
inhaling the common air.
She has no idea what we've been through.

The Teacher and the Prostitute

At home, his lesson plans done,
she tells him of the man
who likes to bend over
and how he likes her just to watch.
"I tell each one he's the greatest
I've ever seen—
great in size, experience, natural style
and even reputation.
'I could even make your reputation'
I told this one very important citizen
just before he played the chicken
& cooed like a dove."

At night she rocks him in bed
when she's home
and continues on with
the stories of her johns
who are, lately, fancy fat cats
but they're still johns, she says,
like anyone else,
someone in pants.

"There's one who likes to be bled
pinprick, pressure,
then touch his wound
and he's all swoons and
'do it again mommy.' "
She tells this tale in a monotone
as he starts to drift—
so she shakes him awake
and sits up on naked knees
very erect,
the body of a grown child,
and he's alert, very.
"They're all different, the ones who come to me
you know."

He knows:
each day by 9
his room is ordered & receiving
in the derelict school
where he teaches.
By night, after all his young stars
have gone home,
he knows everything she says
and how ravenous she is
for a listener like him.

They Say

the homeless
are tearing apart the bridges
in new york city.
Their need for firewood outstrips
the bridges' capacity to give.

Consider phantom bridges,
darkened dangerous roadways,
feeder roads going nowhere,
and the fires being kept
and everyone
warm along the waterfront,
under the rusting trestles
of this fine city.

Gone are the great and graceful spans of light.

Action:
the iron helmets need to know:
which of you
pulled the wood down,
who handed what to whom,
who was there to strike the match;
how many shielded the small flame
and fanned it larger?
How many spent the night?
The failed bridges are losing memory.

Beneath the few still grand remaining spires,
there is less;
more and more—this new milling life,
a flickering band
girding the city.

Hungry Dogs

A pack of mongrels,
having picked the city clean,
limps to the border
to where they've never been.

A month has passed
since the last blast and spear of weaponry;
the last fire is out.

(ah! the corners, the back alleys
what all went down in the districts)

You can see their ribs now
through their fur, which
still shines in any light,
like
the punishing light of the sun.

Hungry—see them bite the air
and sniff about
the imprints.
Where are those human bodies now?
Who did the moving?

Perspective

Were I not part of us
how carefully I would point us out: you on the telephone
and him on a lounge a hundred miles away.
I'd be jealous of both—you breaking the rules
and his complicity.
But I'm here, in front of you
involved, as it were,
in the evening;
my arms around your knees
my head for you to hold or consider.

It took a great mounting of natural events—
earthslides, mushroom growth,
before I'd slide my cheek up this way
or lose a burden this way.

If I were not part of us
I'd imagine sanctions and flight.

Her Complex

What do you say to her,
all alone in a velvet room
as if she'd never been the crack
in the center of a crowd,
enthralled?
And how do you reach her
outward wings and carrying. . .

Settle down boy.

Visiting, over wine,
she says she suffers
(her wings shimmering,
eyes pencilled and hot)
an inferior complexity.
Wrong, I say,
your complexity is no easy matter:

You don't bump into things,
and they still fall.

She/He Lost   *for Kath*

lost   how easily
(glide on grease)
she could become —seize—
she would seize the collar
of lost
diamonds every inch around
her sparkling neck

that tightening collar
the soft leather feels just
fine and then
after a slow cigarette,
a song
she's gone.

Hearts

How does your love grow
my love?
I mean for another.
His photo, the other day shown off
in the middle of our moves,
minutes before we brushed,
was not enough for me
and more than enough.

Wild, I think maybe
he could be wild with you;
he could be wily too in my mind
and forgetful.
But he doesn't lodge there,
nor in my heart
—though I'm still in your house.

And his heart is gone,
lost already and wrapped around you.
Do you know this for sure?
Do you know his heart?
You smile that you know.
What else do you need to know?

Loving the Moon

Out of love's arms
according to law
& how we finally followed it.
I, struck & dulled,
see the old moon stray,
spraying light across
a field of clover.

So, I'll love the moon a while,
so white & armless;
nothing to fold into,
nothing to smell.
Silent, prideless moon,
has no need to stamp, grind
or smack about.
I'll neither hook it
nor lightly pierce
its moving shades.

Jessie at 8

She concentrates on her dentistry.
She may give up the trade and its tools tomorrow,
but for now, she's engaged,
operating on two old jaws.
One is a deer's
and that's the youngest,
the freshest dead.
"The spaces between the teeth
are perfect," she says.
She pokes and picks around. She says,
cleaning out the plaque,
"Gee your plaque is big" —
a certain way of talking to animals
dead or alive — friendly.

The second set of teeth is darker,
petrified, hoary with age.
No visible spaces between those dentures;
not enough jaw to identify.
She doesn't flinch
but speeds ahead to improve
what's left of a mouth.

She looks up:
"I'm the dentist of dead animals."

Some Towns; Even Cities

Through some towns
Death the jaded jockey
presses more tightly
on his spurs.
The horse literally flies.
Eyes shut rather than behold
such misrule.
Children become matches,
little sulphur heads
struck by a design.

(The local gentry, the polite ones,
invite The Monster for dinner.
They let him rest in their midst.
They arm him for battle.
And The Monster, having eaten well,
eats them too.)

The hamlet, the village,
even the city—some cities,
know that when it feels bad
soon it's going to smell bad.
IT—the clouds smile down
and gather quickly:
they expel some new hardware
no ordinary cloud could fathom.
There is no boasting in the heavens
at such times.

Talking to the Wind

I'm talking to the wind again
(not softly in this tumult)
and to the fiery demons of my dreams;
and the wind has no ears
and the wind is blind
with no mouth to turn down at the corners.

Outside, under the eaves and the flapping shade,
I blast my curse into its coming wake.
Words barely said are sucked into the backdraft.

Should I leave off?
I've talked to what has left me.
I've fought against the rush
over my right shoulder.

When the wind dies, I'll calm down,
apolitical, dozing.
But in my sleep
there's a deft skipper
I need to talk to,
who, like the wind,
scuttles freely across the fields.

Brain Damage

I can go to the spigot and turn it on.
I can drink from it.
With the hose I can moisten the garden
when it's dry,
but I haven't the 8 or 9 words
that go with spigot,
words plumbers and poets must know.

So here too I'm the skimmer
hitting lightly and then
that sinking feeling.
My mind is damaged on the end of the world,
and I'm left only words
like drink and sprinkle and sparkle and spigot.

On a moonless night in the garden
I can no longer name the bright stars
or the iridescent things that fly,
but I can still feel
the hard shell of a snail
and the softer, ordinary slug.

49

The Mouth

A giant mouth leans over the railing
of the George Washington Bridge,
and as it draws the river's surface into its maw,
the crowd, for miles, gasps.

A small fleet of helicopters
drones above the water
almost rippling the disappearing sheen.

The mammoth mouth finally swallows,
and after a basso belch
it changes, as in the movies,
into a passable human form.
All the others
pop back into their cars
and roll off.

With the choppers gone
the hum becomes the normal one
of a normal day—
but the top of the Hudson
is duller than dull can figure,
and nothing reflects there—
and all who are near the banks
or crossing the bridges,
are thoughtless now,

even as the mouth changes again,
grows large and casts about with hunger.

III.   A SCREAM FOR CHARLES TYLER

In Memoriam

One Legged Man

Don't pity the one legged man
for in the face of what binds us all,
the loss of a limb,
like stomach distress,
is but a bruise on the rump of death.

A Scream for Charles Tyler

> No one tells him where to go.
> No one tells him where he's been.
> He tells both softly,
> laid back deliberately
> against his scream
>   Yaaaahoooooooh!

>   Take three notes. . . on top of
>   Take three notes. . . on top of
>   Three more notes. . . a formality.
>   A fist of powder.
>   Muffled scream.

The screamer's voice is sanctioned by style.
The right bolt slides into place.
All he's ever known gathers,
finds one note
(high C)
and is released.

The screamer sits bolt upright,
something new now on his mind:
a melody in the upper register—
fame in the right pitch.

A look at history.
Onward and—
          catch as catch can.

Complaint

The world's been destroying me
with its notions
about my potions
and the ways to my pain.

Shall I shoot myself
backwards
or ahead,
down and under?

Surely
you know
nothing is illegal
at the center of pain
In my pocket there's heaven,
so please,
Mr. Cheese,
leave off!

Careful Bump

I was standing around
figuring my situation
keeping to myself, outside of trouble,
when this guy bumps me

Whammo!

Hey! I say,
watch it,
be more careful!

Careful? he says, why I'm so careful
I don't even see you.

Then I understood my situation:
The casual error of a bump,
chance collisions
set me up
and
let me down.

Footprints

She walks into my footprints
curious everywhere I go
which means
she's been treating me
too one-way.

Every time my mouth falls open
she's in it
every time I suggest now
she's against it
and whenever I have fever
yes, in the middle of my fever,
she takes my heat
and claims it for her own
sweet own.

She's got a bulldog
a pack of friends
and a scar
and not one of those things
treats me with consideration!

I don't know
if I'll ever get out of here
alive.

Birthday Poem

Where you've walked out no one's been.
It could be on an ice cap,
all white sheen, tundra to the horizon,
or by some woodland grove,
no humankind,
only the voices of wild animals
in the egg-like silence of your day.
These murmuring animals know you.

Do you know how fast you breathe
and for how many people?

Meet me in the curve of your hip
my darling,
a cool presence,
a warm presence
                when you're known.

Meet me in the curve of your. . .
                I wish you long life.

Meet me in the curve of your. . .
                I wish you vision around corners.

Meet me in the curve of your. . .
                I wish you courage.

Meet me in the curve of your. . .
                I wish you what you wish.

I wish I wish. . .

                your hips
                your tongue
                driving me
                and my honey
                mad.

Fireball

I want to be a ball of fire
lasting beyond the firefight
brighter than the blazing light
my eyes have always known.

The hot spot in the center swirls,
I imagine, and is indifferent
to the slightly cooler surrounding
liquid/gaseous, impossible to describe
fire.

My footfalls print black
and smoldering.
An elm just burned where I passed.
Soon, nothing within my range
or appetite.

Anger

When anger falls on the plate like food
limp—something you wouldn't
want to eat—don't force yourself
I tell myself
let it go
the feeling of being pissed off
having been ripped off on the run
taken for a fool
some no count lame ass crier
couldn't put a shoe in a basket on a bet
or control his own best leads
a shame to his hours
sucking on anger.

Listen, I tell myself
spit that juice
into waters widening
where the elements in waves
will wash harmless
that wrath,
the truest feeling.

A Lonely Tree

There are 12 men in the toaster
don't ya know
there are 12 men near broiling.

You should do something, but no,
the size of the men
or the size of the toaster
worries you—you talk about it
and draw into yourself
don't ya know.

Elsewhere, but not far,
there are meetings in The Emergency.
Questions spin around broiling:
should a group of heroes
unplug the gadget
which took years of money to build?
If the 12 were set free,
who would they join,
where would they settle?

Would they run to the tree
to save the cat
caught in the branches,
terrified and dangerous to pull down?

You pull yourself together
and laugh.
12 men in a toaster
don't ya know
and cat's in a tree—true.

The temperature's broiling
and the mice, they've disappeared
don't ya know.

Where I Need to Be

Crystal coke and fine mist wine
Is where I need to be.
The devil took the lesser soul
And left the skin for me.

In fallow fields of discontent
The braggart devil lies.
His fists are tight, his movements light,
And watch how well he dies.

He comes again to take a spine,
To take a leaf and leave a stain.
His death is but a parody
of dying grief beneath the pain.

So it's cold
Beneath the wind,
And it's where I want to be,
And crystal coke
And fine mist wine
Are all that's left for me —
For the devil took the fattened soul
And left just skin for me.

Rescue

Your hand
         across the water
         on its course —
its reach
         how it comes over
         to my side —
Does it signify
what I need
         transport?
Or is what I see
the dull familiarity of rescue?

Tremulous
         my sigh bumps the rail
         till steady.
Steady
         your grasp there
         is taken.

Fingers now recall the net
for some fish I'm not!
Why are you here
         ringless
         bare wrists
         arms?

Yes, I'm close
Yes, I'm over.

In the Moneytalk

Money talks.
Listen to the sound of the man
who sneaks in his pants,
sneaks by the jewelry store,
by the telegraph office.
There he holds up the wires and gags the man.
He says: money talks —
give me your jewels or your life.
He takes the jewels, makes the switch,
returns and cuts throats to the tune of millions.
The movies love it.

Money talks nobody walks.
He sneaks out the store,
no one is speaking,
coins jingle jangle.
Money he smiles at and money talks back:
I've given you my life, now you give me yours.

No danger in it really,
he'll get down
and cut someone for change
in the moneytalk.

Do It Now

There was one last shot
        in my most loved gun
and the blue glass bottle
        glinted in the sun
thirty yards off,
        secure in the crook of a crab apple tree.

I looked down the blue glass from gunsight.
To hit it now or later?

Now feels right,
        but tomorrow's Sunday,
and I may want
        that Sunday feeling.

So I saved the shot,
went to bed,
        and in my sleep
the gun went off
        —I never heard it.
Next morning I was out of shot
and the blue glass still unshattered.

Next time, I'll take my shot
        first thing,
and get that feeling
        early.

And Now for the Music

There's a terrible rhythm bearing down
a boy with a drum and a permanent frown
a mask on the wall which won't go away
no matter where you move
no matter how you pray.

Imagine—wearing the mask that haunts you.

So the devil floats up off the map of crime
the expensive coat and a $5 shine;
he walks and he talks to the beat of the drum
in the hands of the boy bashing,
sweating, and not yet done.

He's average in the music, he's new
and doesn't know, this time, what to do.

But the devil does and does his dance
arrhythmic jolts in the cuts of chance;
he forgets the boy who beat the drum
in the last few hours
of the blasted sun.

Thus the world comes down
at the end of the day
in the woods—the fields
where animals play;
where men like tigers
act like spiders
weaving about, breathing upon
their ghost-like prey.

RIDGEWAY PRESS BOOKS

1974   Thundershowers Rain On Me Supreme,
       Carl Aniel & Jim Jarvi
1975   The Martyr of Pig,
       M.L. Liebler*
       Knit Me A Pair of Your Shoes,
       John M. Marino & M.L. Liebler*
       Kitano-Po, An Anthology of
       Detroit Writers
1976   Earthwalkers, An Anthology
       of Detroit Writers
       Unfinished Man in the Perfect Mirror,
       M.L. Liebler*
       The Fountain Poems,
       David Burkhardt
       Leonid,
       Robert Coleman
1979   Island from Fear/Critical Chairs,
       Carl Aniel & Gregory Hallock
1980   Measuring Darkness,
       M.L. Liebler
1982   Save The Frescoes That Are Us:
       A Detroit Tribute to Jack Kerouac,
       Edited by M.L. Liebler &
       Edie Kerouac-Parker
1985   Whispers by the Lawn (Exit Back) -
       Volume One,
       M.L. Liebler*
1986   After All,
       Errol Henderson
       Whispers by the Lawn (The
       Twilight Blues) - Volume Two,
       M.L. Liebler
1987   Hideout Matinees,
       Lawrence Pike
       Convalescence and Other Poems,
       Tyrone Williams (Second
       Printing - 1989)
       To William S. Burroughs,
       Edie Kerouac-Parker
1988   Arrivals/Departures,
       Alinda Wasner
       Something in G-Minor,
       Kathleen Meade
       Shirts and Shaved Arm Pits,
       Rudy Baron
       Wearing Doors Away,
       Alise Alousi
       We Just Change The Beat,
       John Sinclair (Second Printing)
       The Form It Takes,
       Stephen Leggett
       Weather Report,
       Keith Taylor
       To Track The Wounded One:
       A Journal,
       Donald Mager
       Breaking the Voodoo & Other
       Performance Poems (cassette),
       M.L. Liebler
1989   Etudes in Wanton Nesses,
       Faruq Z. Bey
       The Evidence of Spring,
       Anca Vlasopolos
       Home During A Dry Spell,
       Jan Worth
       Drifting the Deadlands,
       Michael Delp
       Inheritance,
       Adele Dumaran
       The Hurt,
       Jim Gustafson
       Work (And All That Jazz),
       Susan Smiley

       Collected Poems,
       Jose' Garza
       Toward a Ratio-Nal Aesthetic
       (Music Theory),
       Faruq Z. Bey
       Draft Dodger,
       Eugene Chadbourne
       Skilled Trades,
       Danny Rendleman
1990   The Violence of Potatoes,
       Faye Kicknosway
       snakecrossing,
       Lolita Hernandez
       Blood M Ther,
       Lorene Erikson
       Salad in August,
       Stella L. Crews
       Conformities,
       Laurence W. Thomas
1991   Pierced by Sound,
       Lawrence Pike
       Home Before Light,
       Cheri Fein
       (US)
       Michael Castro
       Bearing Witness,
       Bob Hicok
       The Lingo of Beer,
       Rudy Baron
       A Passionate Distance,
       Joan Gartland
       Gittin Down:
       An Anthology of Prison Writings
       The Cursive World,
       Marc J. Sheehan
       Deliver Me,
       M.L. Liebler
       Labor Pains,
       Edited by Leon Chamberlain
1992   Stations of the Cross
       John R. Reed
       A Modern Fairy Tale:
       The Baba Yaga Poems,
       Linda Nemec Foster
       Listen To Me,
       Faye Kicknosway
       Hacking It,
       Jim Daniels
       On A Good Day,
       Gay Rubin
       de KANSAS a CALIFAS & back to CHICAGO,
       Carlos Cortez
       Mystical,
       Dalmatian
       Deer Crossing/Leap Years Away,
       William Boyer
       Fragile Visions,
       Josef Bastian
       Raking the Gravel & Other Poems,
       Ben Bohnhorst
       Macro-Harmonic Music Manuscript Workbook,
       Faruq Z. Bey
1993   Hunger And Other Poems,
       Geoffrey Jacques
       Mysterious Coleslaw,
       Pamela Miller
       Still Life With Conversation,
       Rebecca Emlinger Roberts
       The Short Life of The 5 Minute Dancer,
       Barry Wallenstein

*Out of Print